Heal Your Love

LUNA MERBRUJA

BIYUTI PUBLISHING

Toronto

biyuti publishing
https://publishbiyuti.org

Cover art by Mar Pascual
Illustration art and image descriptions by Roxana Dhada
Book design by Luna Merbruja
Edited by Maliha Ahmed and Adrían Díaz

First Edition

Praise for *Heal Your Love*

"How do you manifest yourself whole? How do you nurture what was attempted to be buried? *Heal Your Love* offers up a lineage, a love, a spell, and most importantly, a futurity hardly ever promised to a brown trans femme. Luna Merbruja evokes the imperfect majesty of living & loving in every page. *Heal Your Love* proves to be a divine collection– an altar to your Crazy, to your Other, to your Magic. They take precise care in each verse, renewing traumas with milk & honey, declaring boundaries & ancestry with a clear, powerful voice. Merbruja knows of the roses they deserve & this collection will stand for nothing less. Know that you are blessed to witness this kind of birth. So shall it be." — kiki nicole, Poet and Artist

"*Heal Your Love* is the work of a mighty sorceress – a book borne out of the brutality and violence that makes forgiveness oh so tender. Luna Merbruja is a confessional poet whose mastery of the form belies a word-witch at the height of her powers: These poems are life and death and rebirth made into song and spell. Merbruja reaches deep into the genre of memoir, pull out its guts, and shows us the beating heart of what it means to struggle, survive, and thrive as a Brown trans woman in America. These poems are blood, memory and fire. Read these poems." — Kai Cheng Thom, author of *Fierce Femmes and Notorious Liars: A Dangerous Trans Girl's Confabulous Memoir*

"This painfully–yet relievingly–real and aesthetically composed collection is an ardent, heart-felt narrative about resilience, vulnerability, overcoming, nourishment, and becoming. This collection becomes a tale of learning about understanding, forgiveness, and acceptance in all its forms. This insight into the world of a promising multi-platform artist leaves her readers filled with a deeper appreciation for the individual's journey through self-love, healing, and metamorphosis." — Adrián Díaz, Writer and Editor

"Luna Merbruja's work makes me want to live. This book of poetry is the gentlest whisper, telling me that healing is possible, love is worth it, and our imagination is our freedom. Luna has given birth to possibility. I am honored to have witnessed it." — xoai pham, Poet

"Luna's poems are powerful and poignant explorations of love, sex, desire, and identity. She tells truths that are valuable both because they are so often not heard and also because of the stunning level of craft she brings to story-telling." — Nia King, author of *Queer and Trans Artists of Color Vol I and II*

Gratitudes

Gratitude upon gratitude to Adrían Díaz and Maliha Ahmed for editing these poems with precision and style, and all the affirmations that built my confidence.

Gratitude to Nina Simone, Kai Cheng Thom, KOKUMO, and Mark Aguhar for all the inspiration while writing these poems.

Gratitude to all the friends, audiences, strangers, and lovers who rejuvenated me when I wanted to quit.

Gratitude to the #WeLoveLuna support team — Lexi Adsit, Maliha Ahmed, Jo/Chillóna, Nina Malaya, Aurelia Mercer, Devi Peacock, Naomi Masako Reagan, Natasha Simpson, Amita Swadhin — that kept me alive to see this book through.

Gratitude to you, dearest reader, for supporting my work. I hope these words can offer comfort and reflection as tokens of my appreciation.

"I may be crazy but that don't make me wrong."

– Marsha *Pay It No Mind* Johnson

This book is dedicated to

Mark Aguhar,

trans sex workers,

and femmes of color taken by suicide.

There's a home for us after we die.

Contents

Fates and Futures

Prophecy

This spirit
most resilient
element

Tracing Trauma

[Image description: A body with shaded skin is embracing and emerging from a dark vertical oval shape. A twisted spiral staircase shape extends from the bottom to the top of this oval and is broken into bright irregular shards as it meets the body of the figure holding it. At the bottom of the oval, a dollar floats out of a wine bottle stoppered by a baby pacifier. The figure has eyes closed and is turning to look down at another person on the ground below them. The figure's hair is dark and short and pierced by shards emerging from their head. A cloud floats from the oval shape into the figure's hair, and a small childlike body with long hair rests on this cloud.

Below the oval is another shaded person mirroring the figure above them, they are reaching out toward each other. This person's eyes are wide open. They are sitting on a thin layer of dollar bills, fanned out in a half circle under their hips. Bright shards radiate from their thigh and torso and their skin is as dark as the other figure's. A snake wraps around their mouth and head and curls around to face them, it's mouth open and fangs visible. In their hand they are grasping a leather belt that ends in a metal buckle. The belt curls upward intertwining with the snake, a flowering vine, and a segmented cord that curl all the way up to the second figure's mouth and ear. Together these lines make a spiraling shape that mirrors the spiral within the oval.]

My Mother In Frozen Memories

i didn't want to have a kid in high school.
carrying an A-named child, perfect for my Scarlet stomach.
all the judgmental glares, my mother too far too gone to care.
a world like this makes a stone tomb of your womb.

the narcissist signed the birth certificate seeing his name twice.
like clockwork, left me for another woman
just like he left another pregnant woman for me.
didn't pay for diapers, binkies, or blankets
and had the nerve to tell my son i was on welfare when i busted my ass
off finishing school,
where i met my gay best friend who got me a job working full-time at
pizza hut.

my child looks just like his dead beat biological father,
those words i fed him with scoops of gerber.
he has the things i hate about myself —
my snakebite fast wit, broad nose,
and stubbornness to always be right.

monkey doesn't see his father, but still does what he does.
catch him smiling the same charming way,
cracking jokes and swooning hearts.
growing into a handsome boy that chooses to be a tender feminine
faggot.

it's his godfather's fault his dead beat biological father says.

i agree, but only in private.

i accept gays as long as they aren't my kids.

sometimes it hurts seeing how much love he needs.

he hugs strangers and holds hands,

likes to sit next to me and pick under my fingernails.

i yelled at him once because he picked too deep

and he never did it again.

i don't know how to tell him i miss it.

as he grows i keep missing him.

i can only hug him after i beat him,

only tell him i love him after i bruise him;

loving him in the way i saw my father love my mother.

he flinches at me.

> *how dare he*
>
> *i am his mother*
>
> > *not a monster*

i beat this into him.

  can't he see that i, too, cry as i bring down the belt?

no, he's hiding in his clothes, reaching for the blanket.

  when i ask him to look at me,

i'm not sure he can see with all that drama pouring out his face.

i can't be a monster.

i buy him elotes and Gap,

still take him to school most days even though he looks like his Dad.

i have no control over my life.

this child is the most wild thing,

a lion of love i can only tame with a whip.

i hate myself for birthing him into this world.

i asked his father for $500 towards an abortion.

instead, kept both the money and the baby.

II

i gave this child breath,

frozen foods, a new place every few months, a good life.

but he's ungrateful.

i see he cuts his arm now, got skinny.

hides behind black self-dyed bangs and patchy bleach jobs.

listens to rocker music with eyes glued to the computer screen.

my cousin caught him posting photos of himself

wrapped in towels on myspace;

he'd posted something public that hinted about being raped.

12 years old and my child is Going Through It.

he can tell hundreds of strangers on the internet

as if his own mother doesn't have a heart.

when i confront him, he has that blank stare.

                                               denies everything // deletes everything

i try to beat the lies out of him but he won't confess

  and we don't talk about it again.

i don't know how to take care of him or what to make of him.
this lion strong enough to bite the whip out of my hand,
hardened heart too impervious to feel my fists pounding it.

my last line of defense is this serpent's tongue

Drama Queen / faggot pussy bitch / emo little shit

listen hear me look at me
   answer me *mira* do you understand?
      underneath all this monstrosity is a failed mother.

i know he hates me too.
see it in how he half-asses every chore,
rolls his eyes and mutters under breath when he spends more
   than a minute with family.
carries books to hide away, living in his head full of smarts.
as a freshman starts working and paying his own
   phone bill and bus pass,
the only kid out of five siblings that doesn't get a ride to school.
spends more time there and at work than home.
starts doing those overnight trips, flying all over the country to
   places i've dreamed of visiting.
doesn't even ask permission anymore, just tells me he'll be gone a
   few days
packing up that green Ciao suitcase he's had since he was five.

IV

i'm missing him all the time now.

i was too broke to celebrate his 15th birthday,

his auntie and godfather took him to San Francisco instead,

fed him and loved him in ways money can.

on his 16th he was on a plane to D.C. doing god knows what —

i don't know him anymore.

he comes back radiant for a few days, then

hides behind school, work, and books until a few weeks later he

   f l i e s   a w a y   again

               finding happiness everywhere outside our nest.

V

i couldn't do it anymore.

had to give him up.

sent him to his father's mother's house, where everyone

is given their own bedroom and $20 bills for lunch money.

a house where favorite foods are kept in the fridge, where

   delicious meals are made fresh every night.

everyone sits together at a table,

   talks to each other with smiles and jokes

            like they truly want to be there.

from this safe distance, i can feel my anger.
hiding it in my remaining three kids' pockets where a social worker
won't find it.

from this safe distance, he calls
and confesses to me for the first time that his cousin raped him.
his sense is lost somewhere between gusts of sobs
and i have none to spare.
i tell him *everything's going to be okay*
hold on, i'll call you back.
i write a letter to our family telling them what happened,
telling them to choose a side, that they won't see him again,
and how could we have let this happen?

there's no longer a safe distance.
                    i am a failed mother / i am a monster
all this child — all my child has known is pain.
  wasn't he smiling? happy? laughing?
could he survive this better than i can?
i remember my sister doing this to me but my mom didn't listen.

i believe my own kid.

i call him back and he's crying heavy begging to come home.
i feel the electrocution through the telephone line, but
i tell him *no,*

                    two broken generations won't make a whole.

i take him to the police station,
sit next to him as the officer asks questions
while i wish he didn't have answers.

VII

we lost the case.

my son is Gay and our family thinks he asked for it.

the judge ruled that we surpassed the statute of limitations.

we

waited

too

long

...

VIII

we're on the phone, he's heading off to college in a month.

he says he doesn't want us to visit his dorm,

i call his bullshit and say,

you don't want our ghetto asses to embarrass you, huh?

my anger is a jealousy.

he finally ran away, gets to re-create himself and start anew.

forget all of us who sacrificed for his becoming,

like the dreams i awoke from to break my back supporting him.

how i stayed with men who beat me to provide him dinner to eat.

how could i have better taught gratitude into him?

i've told him many times,

he is all i have.

the only consistent thing in my life,

an evasive lion who looks way too much like my first heartbreak.

that should have been enough forewarning.

i receive his e-mail.
he's been raped, supposedly.
dropped out of college.
tried to kill himself again.

what can i do?
there's not enough love in all our generations
to fill the brokenness he inherited.

he tells me he's my daughter now, and
he won't come back unless
i swallow my disapproval

my God and my Heart
don't believe in his sickness

We can't save him

X

seven years silence

he's a scale

     his happiness heavier than

          my loneliness

he is full

     in abundance of love

          cared for by faggots

             all across this country

i kept him at a distance

and now it's permanent.

Alcohol

2 months into Al-Anon
almost learned the Serenity Prayer
something like:

Dear God,
I ask that you give me the strength to change the things I can,
accept the things I cannot,
and the wisdom to know the difference.

in a car ride from Riverside to Mountain House
i hear *0 to 100 / The Catch Up*
think of Jewelio, think of liars
think of my father
pouring beer into a yellow-tinted Squirt bottle before the movie
pouring vodka and orange juice into the green thermos before
    the flea market

Grandma and Robert pouring one bottle of wine in their glasses
    every night with or without dinner
Grandma smiles, laughs louder, babbles that she loves me
Robert reddens, tongue snarky, hips greased enough to dance

Vinny drinks a baby's weight in Budweiser
slicing me with threats, some deep enough that
grandma calls the police only to tell them once they show up,
"Esta bien, es OK, he's calm and sleeping now."

Time Traveling Through Trauma

No machinery required
utilizing skin as blanket
i pull it over my eyes and sleep my way
back to the little girl colored invisible

We spend time prancing with dolls
letting her wear makeup while playing video games
marathoning Pokémon with her favorite french toast breakfast
an eternal Saturday morning

There's no rush to wake as she naps on clouds
i spend lifetimes on my hands and knees in bleach and prayer
desperately scraping stains off the inside of her skull

I claw at her brain sometimes
gnawing at the neural networks hoping i can vomit all these
generations of rape-infused DNA memories out

When it gets this bad
this horrendously grotesque
she, my little darling girl, is only further harmed

Screaming at me to stop, leave her be
she claws the skin off my eyes
i see bone wedged under my bloodied nails
see her grown & scarred & beautiful ugly

Beautiful ugly, like time traveling through trauma
like learning how to love my mosaic skull
no longer needing bleaching
just a dancing girl
and her favorite everythings

If Death

[Image Description: The upper portion of an hourglass shape cradles a person's face, their hands crossed at the wrists under their chin. Their skin is shaded with many fine contour lines and is mostly dark. A white scar extends from the right side of their forehead to the center of their nose. Their eyes are closed. In the center of their forehead, a framed vertical oval shape rises upward. Small dots line their hairline and short dark strokes float into their hair, which sweeps off to the right and surrounds the oval shape. The hands have short round nails, mottled skin over the knuckles, and a dark scrape on the left side. Below the hands, the hourglass shape narrows and forms a small circle that contains a small pair of scissors with the blades open. A pale worm emerges from both outer corners of the person's eyelids and their parted lips, and curls down their chin between the open blades of the scissors.

The curved bottom bowl of the hourglass shape is filled with black earth. Four pale worms curl upward through the darkness towards two feet planted halfway into the dirt. The toenails have grown beyond the toes. The skin is mottled in patches along the ankle, heel, joints and sides of the toes. Between the feet, the bulb of a plant extends a handful of roots down and 3 stems up to the surface. Above ground, the stems turn into a single white lily between two dark leaves.]

Goddess Have Mercy

last night i held tight to Clementine
smelled her cotton soaked from tears 3 years ago to 3 weeks ago
wiped my fresh ones onto her belly

i felt warm, safe, soft
in this place i carved out from years of barely surviving

somehow i've created a place to call home
or truthfully, my death bed

i begged goddess to take me
slit my spirit in my sleep
let me bleed into the afterlife
take me
    TAKE me
       TAKE ME

show mercy
i've tried taking myself and nothing dies
smooth scars & keloids lasting evidence of where i've been
    and what i'll return to

I Am 21 Years Old And This Is My Last Will And Testament

if i am murdered
if i take my life
    do not arrest my killer
do not condemn who or what has killed me
    be it a lover or client or survival

if my bio family betrays me in a suit, prints my birth name, and
misgenders me,
    do not publicize it

let my death be unsettling
let it sit in your gut and throat like heavy constipation

hold my killer accountable with gentleness
if possible, ask them *Why?*
                 what has broken within them?

use my decay as fertilizer for healing growth
allow my murderer to sift through the ashes of my body where
    my hands once held their gentleness
    my dimples once held their laughter
    my feet once raced through their thoughts enticing, enticing until i
was no more

let the murderer feel what is mine, finding clues to their crime
uncovering that in killing me they mortally wounded themself
a sin unearthing two graves: for my body and their future

let them be at my death ceremony

let me say *thank you, goodbye*

and make peace with the reaper who blessed me with afterlife

treasure my bones and burn my flesh

let me live in an essence after death

eternally i sleep soundly, dream lucidly —

                                        an end to chronic nightmares

just blissful sweetness con amigas during sunset

an abundance of the absences in my living

from the grave

do not put me on the TDOR list
do not let white people make art of me
do not tell my parents

let me rot *sin* embalming fluid
organize immediately upon death
fundraise for familia across the globe
bring them to my decay, then
let us pray

my open casket a family reunion
meet each other for the first or four hundredth time
drink my favorite:
orange juice, horchata, jamaica, milkshakes
        all thick in authenticity

write your goodbye wishes on my flesh
spells for crafting femme futures
watch them,me,everything burn
scatter us over the free ocean

plant a rose bush in memory of my sweet thorns

                                    i'm with our Stonewall mothers now

for the women who don't get to be girls

i know it's not the case, but i wish in your final moments
you knew you were loved.

i wish his hands didn't choke the life out of you,
wish the knife wasn't stabbed into you twenty-two times,
wish you weren't drowned in a toilet,
or filled with cum when he shot you in the head.

i know it's not the case, but you didn't need to be a headline
the seventh
or
thirteenth
or
twenty-sixth
counter on a year that won't fucking end.

and when it does,
the counter begins again
like the sole consistency is in our death
like each victory is recoiled with seven sacrifices

i'm sorry that even in memory,
your womanhood is robbed
you are deadnamed and misgendered and fodder
for wannabe feminist websites, paying cis people to write your story
while the streets remain empty
when millions marched for women
(which women did they march for?)

i'm sorry people don't see you as victims of
intimate partner violence, as victims of
sex trafficking, as victims of
reproductive justice's negligence
(how can you create families when the mothers are murdered?)

during this genocide i wish we could take up arms
replace our teeth with bullets,
our knuckles with diamonds,
lace our nails with poison,
and our glares with medusa's protection

i wish i could cast a resurrection spell for every
woman who didn't get to be a girl
for us to be elders who lived through
their second puberty, adolescence, and adulthood

i wish i could time travel to every last breath
and breathe flowers into your wounds
close your eyes with the softest rose petals
and guide your spirit to a place
where you are free
and in love
and

alive

Learning Love

[Image description: A figure facing off the page to the right holds a hand up to their forehead, their dark hair swept back behind them. Their skin is shaded with contour lines. A white snake rises up from the center of their chest to below their ear, its lower body drapes over their right shoulder. Short dark thorns float from the body of the snake to the figures throat and into the air in front of their face. Multiple arms radiate from their bent elbow below the snake. One arm reaches behind them holding long, sharp scissors, cutting off one of two long dark braids. One arm holds the lower braid, and another arm uses the end of a braid to write a letter behind the figures back. The letter is stuck in their garter belt under a peach. Two other arms extend in front of the figure, unbraiding a braid halfway, the ends of which are wavy and separate into strands.

Below their arm along the side of their torso, there are visible creases in their flesh indicating where their belly, hips, and thighs expand. There are two flower shapes with thorns in place of their nipples. There is a thorny flower pattern over their crotch and along the line of their hips. Their erection extends upward beyond the pattern. On their belly, 5 dark small fetuses are visible, the cords wrapping behind their erection. One of their hands rests on a skull with its tongue out tasting their thigh, there is a short sword stabbing through their hand and the skull.]

Three Times Perfect

I was a few months shy of the legal 18, in the hot boredom of Central California in the between of high school and college.

I began a new hobby – internet cruising for sex.

I was young with the power of Google Search to decipher

DDF   MWM   CD   TS   M4M   M4T

I was scared horny, lonely and new.
Easy prey for this gay rite of passage into predatory grounds that was about to devour me,

and it did.

Beginning with 47 year-old Craig, a white man who piloted private jets to Lake Tahoe and Reno and San Diego.

Who called me on the phone and asked me

my age   my interests   my race   my address

and I gave it all to him.

When he knocked on my front door,
I opened it with fearful hope to cure this summer boredom.

Craig was the first.
Holding my thighs to his lips, whispering to my scars,
"You are perfection."

He rolled his tongue over those most vulnerable parts of me
and I quivered hard until

I came.

   and I sent him home
    and I washed my uncle's bedding
     and I sat in my sickened silence.

T. Dancer. Academic.

House sitting in Redwood City where the grass is green and the poor
people are elsewhere.

What was I doing in this neighborhood?

Visiting. Young. Queer.
Wanting someone to see me as anything other than male,
I thought he would have that vision.

He had lust-heavy vision, the second person to call me perfect.

Touching my body before the shower,
in midday sunlight standing inside someone else's kitchen,
He said my small lumps of breasts were feminine,
my brown smooth skin layered like Earth,
my eyes shaped like pensiveness

                              deep and knowing

                                                       hurt.

He grabbed my ass, again, called me perfect.
Said my thighs were thick and hard like Aztlán.
The desired mix of indulgence.

He held my face
Perfect
through the vision of seeing me male.

Jewelio, not Julio, but Jewelio.
Bored white Italian whose Virgo sign made for magnetic explosive sex
with my heavily demanding Libra self.

He said if he could live in the heat of my pussy and dick,
    he would.

Starved was he for a t-girl like me, enduring 5 days of my
            DANGEROUS   HELLISH   ANGER
to suck the fruit and its juice tucked in my panties once more.

The third time he was invited into my mermaid cove,
I gave him my sweetest taste.
Lingerie fresh from a visiting techie sugar daddy,
I knew I had awakened the power of my body and sex.

He kissed me gently,   scared,   just like every straight man
I've ever had the displeasure of blessing.

He licked from neck to stomach, stopping at my lace garter thong where
my blooming cock began poking out the top.

He kissed my crotch, fingers *s l o w l y* pulling down my panties
as my clit slapped him in the face.
He ran his hands up my flat chest and whispered,
"You're perfect."

Yes, I am.

I know I'm perfect.

Three times perfect.

Perfect brown boy fetish.

Perfect tranny fetish.

Perfect whore.

Three Times Perfect.

The kind of perfection that your cum dreams of,
my body that   feeds you,   grows you,   satiates your cravings.

You want three times perfection.

Perfect
enough
to fuck
but not
enough
to love.

If I give you perfection, *what the fuck are you gonna give me?*

sometimes a lonely witch wants you to miss her

when my hair was sixteen inches
i braided three chunks, banded them
then sheared them off as ritual renewal

bald headed, brace-faced, tiny tittied
i wore wigs, timid smiles, & stuffing
wanting for fingers to fill my mouth & cunt

sex an ephemeral calculation
one need plus one fetish equals
an unsatisfactory nothing

tonight i unbraided a chunk
blew hexes into the wind like dandelion seeds
your dick-throbbing thoughts are my target

my orgasms linked to your brain
when i cum you dream of me
a whore's curse upon thy mind

when i fuck, you find new flesh
to project these dreams onto
squeezing eyelids to materialize me

pray and cum harder, honey
let your sadness ooze into your hand
as i sleep alone without a stir

First Dates

when i was 15
my first date with a charming man at P.F. Chang's
led to lots of nervous laughter
charm
vulnerability
and a marriage proposal.
halted by the bland chapstick flavor of his lips
i might have said yes
fulfilling
an old dream of being an ideal wife.

when i was 18
my first date with a polyamorous man was at a café
and i don't drink coffee.
he was thrice my age
offered his hot tub, naked
offered his bed, naked
a ponytail long enough to choke me
should have been a warning for when he would
gag me with slime from a skullfuck.
stayed the night afraid, crying.
woke up to,
"i wish i had a toothbrush for you."

when i was 21

my first date with an empath wearing green contacts

was at a café

and i still don't drink coffee.

ordered peppermint hot chocolate

he paid, i smiled

i laughed, he smiled

he smoked, i avoided

i was honest, he was honest.

best first date.

didn't have a second

because i'm a whore

and he has no love for sloppy seconds.

i'm still 21

last night another first date

with someone's trauma from 3 years ago

who didn't ask questions

who kissed like a fish

who ended the night with

"do you know a motel around here?"

tonight, i'm too jaded for a phone call
where a potential date tells me how
"honored" he is to be dating a writer

wants the prestige
and none of the work
wants the dick
and none of the person
wants the fantasy
and none of the reality

i can't do this anymore.

Reasons why you'll fall in love with me

My smile is kind, inviting,
an open rose plucked from a neighbor's garden.
The warmth in the between of my fingers,
the soothe and soft of my embrace.
I am someone you will trust.

Not loving foolishly,
I love nakedly, unashamedly; lends you to feel powerful
until I bare my claws and fangs.
Initially startled, then hungry with excitement,
I am someone you will lust.

When we kiss, it will taste like clouds
soft, wet, drifting slow and heavy;
as if I'm telling your lips to let go of your ex lover.
When you touch my body I will shiver, shake,
as if warning my flesh cannot tell friend from foe.
I am someone you will be gentle with.

Ice skating fingertips along your scars,
kissing the pores on your face,
licking the heart, tasting your fate.
I can love the You that you don't,
teach how to drop cloth to unveil spirit.
I am someone you will not forget.

Hungry, you are a snake seeking my heat.
Thinking about me when you're not thinking about me.

Call, text, write letters.

Every romantic thing you've ever seen.

I am someone who doesn't choose easily.

Lying in tangled hair and thundering pouring clouds.

Caressing reptilian scales, swallowing sweet need,

soon enough clawing into your back.

You fang my neck

HARDER

at my breathy command.

I am someone who needs roughness.

Love muscle overdrive,

bodies humping, grinding,

necks bent to goddess, breathing mixed moans.

You'll think this is love and I'll think this is pleasure.

I am someone who's learned the difference.

Questioning, doubting yourself.

I am too dreamy a lover, you must be spellbound asleep.

Your spirit leaves and your body stays.

I am somehow Too Good to Be True,

someone worthy of someone better.

We will fight about not communicating,

and then not communicate.

We will sleep with our backs scowling at each other

both hoping the other will cave in.

I will,

and it will only frustrate you.

You are tired of me trekking the extra miles.

You resign to "*You are worthy of someone better.*"

But you are wrong,

leaving me with the intimate carcass of us,

a shovel, and precious stones

that I bury in an unnamed forest with an unmarked grave.

Reasons why you won't

A hunger too massive for my mouth to fit;
I want to swallow the salt of the oceans,
sip the lava of volcanoes, chew the cliffs off every coast.

A hunger this wild is a curse.

Love, are you vast enough for my need?
Can you pick a bouquet of the brightest stars?
Will your poetry be the kind that transcends time,
    future self finding it in an archive and falling in love with you
    all over again?

You might date my trauma before you date me.
I might make commitments I forget.
I don't believe in forevers or fantasies;
make promises that become realities.

I am a girl with limited time, endless eyerolls,
and half a birth chart in air elements.

I am a creature with restless appendages, monstrous moods,
and five babies wrestling in my womb.

I am unloveable until you love yourself.
I am undesirable until you choose yourself.
I am unpredictable until you know yourself.

These are the reasons why you won't love me,
and these are the reasons why I'm glad you don't.

Immunity

I'm a good kisser. I know this
From years of tugging lips and licking spit
When that moan from deep down under
Utters in a breath against my mouth.

I'm a great kisser. I take in your breathy moan
Tasting the shapes of air like the alphabet begging
For more-wet deeper-tongue rougher-bite
And to make sure this breath is clear I ask
"Is this okay?"

"Fuck yes" "mmhmm" "more please"
I lick your earlobe before I whisper
"What stories do you need to tell?"
And like communion wine you pour
Out every sobering truth
You've denied your own self access to.

I drink you in but don't get drunk
My blood thicker from a lineage of alcoholism
My spirit calloused from generational trauma

Your wounds won't break me.

Yet you try
To be heavier than concrete
Try to find a story with enough potency to
Bring me down a notch, push me away
When drinking your poison only draws me closer
Knowing that I am immune

You tell me
It's my turn to bleed a little
You finger my belly button
My *Do Not Touch* spot.
You demand my tears
I've Tried
I'm Trying
What I confess freaks you out
You who descended from family blood thin as money

I sink my fangs into your neck
Ask you to make love to me like you do to your fantasies
You kiss me like you do shame
Kiss me like my face is Medusa's
Can't part your lips to taste my toxic

Not immune

"Is this what you really want?"
You say *"Yes"*
The same way you say yes to your abusive parents
I ask again, *"Are you sure?"*
And it's like you studied for this moment
Read social justice theory for this moment
Want to practice radical love & compassion
In trying to desire a crazy brown trans girl
— just for this moment

I'm tired of relationships that last for a heartbeat
Tired of being your growth catalyst
Of being the mirror to reflect your shortcomings
And the mother's breast you suckle for comfort

I am not frigid
I am not stone
I am flesh and blood and magic
Star hot and volcanic explosive

I want you to believe in my best
To take a bite out my past
And love my poisoned blood like you're immune

But you're not.
Instead
You're repulsed, and yet,
Relying on me to nurse us back to health.

Carlos

"i need you to hold me and watch a movie without having sex"
i text him after a visit with my best friend who's been in a psych hold
the past two days

an hour and a half later after meeting adrienne marie brown at the
Octavia's Brood afterparty in an Oakland shoe store,
where i bought the book and anxiously left
reassuring myself the hour drive home that
it's okay i'm crazy and
get what you need
when you need
what you need

Carlos takes thirty minutes to get to my place
enough time for me to wolf down spaghetti while folding the clothes
strewn across the floor listening to Lianne La Havas foreshadowing
heartbreak

i tell myself i'm going to be comfortable tonight hiding behind layers of
foundation, contour, eyeliner, a bra and cami that exaggerate my itty
bitties,
the rushed decision to throw my wig on no cap and loosely tied even
though my scalp wants to feel some type of love

throughout the night

    his buzzing phone   my bed   our sleepiness naked
                                   not touching

by morning, buzzing waking
he tells his dad "estoy con mi amigo"
when the previous night he called me amiga
i guess he's afraid to tell his parents he's dating
or ashamed of the t-girl he spent the night with
both of which keep me silent & invisible as he hangs up
crawls back into bed without touching any part of my spirit

he shakes me a little,
says it's 5am
he has to go
i sneak him out
come back to a misshapen bed &
a Netflix screen of a movie he picked
because he didn't like anything on My List

i lose my phone
think maybe he accidentally took it
and now i'll never hear from him again
knock over a cup of water in my search, clean it by myself
and it's a simple task that i don't want to do,
or don't want to do alone

i find my phone at 5:48am, no messages or calls

i write this poem on a shred of paper
tuck it into my mattress
cherishing the one thing   that will stay in bed   with me

you earned this

someday, i'll tell you i thought of you during orgasms a few days prior
to the show.
that i processed with a close friend how you're the first queer in a year
i've been with.
my last, an unfaithful ex, a white non-binary trans girl (like you).

except a lot is new,
like my boobs and my cumming and my need to be princess.
my standards for a lover & partner   my barriers   my trust,
and my promise to never date another white person.

i want to go back,
to keep that heat warm in my body when i asked,
i want to go home with you to cuddle and make out,
how do you feel about that?
you said,
yes, yes! absolutely.
the warmth of your bed, me on my stomach, you on your side
hip locked into place stroking my back when i inquired,
what does my body feel like to you?
slowly, sweetly,
like a beach;
skin soft as sand, curves and dips like dunes, deep ocean's beauty.

you empath, you Georgia bred & raised, you cult survivor, you
who remembers my chamomile tea the second morning,
who doesn't laugh when i slip and fall on my ass in the shower with 30

year worn out treads,

who looks me in the eyes at a trans fundraiser and says,

    I want you, Luna

blinking back pessimistic paranoia,

       I want you, too.

like the first night of tired disabled heavy petting kissing cuddling.

too tired to penetrate but you right there at the opening of me.

us moaning the only way we can when you're inside a heat

hotter than intercourse.

how many times can we breathy whisper back and forth

        i want you to fuck me

           i want to fuck you

                i want you to fuck me

                    i want to fuck you

    foreplay-fucking hard and never breaking that boundary?

                      (the answer is *plenty*)

i remind myself this is a summer fling until August when you fly back
across the country to the state you've ironically only seen two peach
trees in.

before you board that plane,

paint my octopus pretty in the bathroom.

i want to carry the bruise of heat and lust,

of body touched memory for a week at least.

i'll give you rose quartz for the journey home.

i'll send a love letter that promises a happy ending,

because neither of us have had a real one of those.

TO THE CIS STR8S WHO WANT A TRANNY

FIRST AND FOREMOST

NO

SECOND

NEVER

THIRD

HA HA HA HA HA HA HA HA HA HA HA HA HA HA HA HA HA HA HA HA HA HA HA HA HA HA HA HA HA HA IS THE SOUND OF MY FAKED ORGASM BECAUSE I AM BORED OF GRINDING AGAINST YOUR MOIST MESS OF A TIRED ATTEMPT OF A FUCK

FOURTH

DON'T HIT ME UP UNLESS YOUR DICK IS BIGGER THAN MINE

FIFTH

DON'T HIT ME UP UNLESS YOUR MOUTH CAN HANDLE A DICK AS BIG AS MINE

SIXTH

NEVERMIND

JUST DON'T HIT ME UP

PERIOD

SEVENTH

YOU REALLY AREN'T ALL THAT SPECIAL OR GREAT

EIGHTH

IM SURE YOUR GIRLFRIEND THINKS THAT TOO

NINTH

WE ARE SMARTER THAN YOU THINK

YOUR GIRLFRIEND AND I

WE ONLY FUCK YOU WHEN OUR VIBRATORS

RUN OUT OF BATTERIES

TENTH

IF I NEEDED DICK I'D USE MY OWN

OR ANOTHER GIRLS'

YOU ARE OBSOLETE

How to Heal

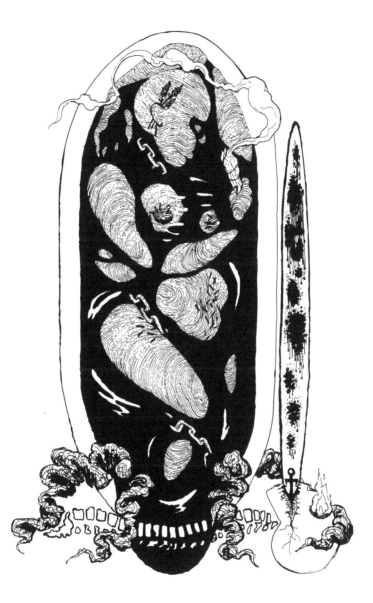

[Image description: A figure floats in an oval bathtub of black liquid, seen from above. Their arms, rounded lower and upper belly, and thigh are visible emerging from the liquid in separated shapes like islands. Their skin is shaded with many fine contour lines and is mostly dark. Three sprigs of lavender are tucked behind their ear and their head is bald. Thick chain links slightly emerge from the surface below their head, next to their hip, and below their knee. One arm is holding a smoking bundle of dried plants. The smoke curls over and behind their head. A few ribs are visible around their breasts, their left nipple is pierced. Small dark short strokes of hair surround their nipples, extend in a vertical line down the center of their belly, and graze the top of their thigh.

They are facing the right side of the bathtub, which is next to a vertical oval mirror that is splattered with black shapes. The bottom of the mirror is wedged in the open mouth of a skull, there is an anchor in the skull's mouth. The skull is attached to a spine that lays horizontal under the tub, and the tub's dark liquid pours over the center of the spine. Four textured entrails emerge from the tub to drape over and around the spine and the skull. The skull's eye socket contains a small fire.]

Transition

after a half dozen dark brown hair dyes to cover the
streaks of moldy green, i shaved my head bald
went to an orthodontist to straighten things out,
got four teeth pulled, then plucked them from the
biohazard box like precious gemstones
took my HRT pills on time, made a spreadsheet
of every symptom from day one to day four hundred
second puberty a mystery unfolding
reshaping my creaturehood beyond recognition

i didn't want to become a woman
it was an accidental shapeshift
i was aiming for beautiful, lovable;
a face my mother could love,
or at least forgive.

i ended up with something else entirely:
lighter skin & looser curls, thicker thighs, tgirl titties
slice-a-man nails, resting bitch face, standoffish attitude
she/her pronouns & tampon coupons, decent dates
frequently complicated relationships
a bisexual (lesbian?) identity, confusion & acceptance

and a wild adventure trans goddesses dreamt for us

What They Don't Tell You About Being Trans

My mouth stretches into smiles far more often these days,
not when men tell me to on the street,
but when I'm taking selfies or people-watching
or painting my nails, feeling femme freedom.

I feel at home in one place I hadn't thought possible – my spirit.
The way I dress my body and cut my hair and fix my face becomes
intentional.
Every choice of adornment is a self-love spell cast for
me, my own, and our future.

Every moment living while trans is a victory.
You are a victory.
Every day, you are a victory.

I didn't know that restrooms would become restless rooms.
Didn't know I could hold my need to pee for three hours,
or that I'd sometimes find a cup
and crawl into my car's trunk because
I was too afraid, too visibly trans to use a restroom.

I didn't know I'd end up looking like my mother,
but better.
I didn't know about first timers' porn fantasies.
Still don't know what people think when they stare at me like,
Are you clocking me?
or, *Do you find me attractive?*
and, *Why are those two separate conclusions?*

Either way, I've become hyperaware of my body.
Foreigner looking from the outside in
ensuring nothing is giving me away,
a futile obsession
when even in my dreams and nightmares
I am myself, trans always.

I didn't know I'd get great at doing my makeup
in the dark
in 15 minutes
in my car
because I wouldn't have a safe place to get dressed.

I didn't know my mother's unconditional love
would become conditional.
That my gender would be the end of our 16 year relationship.

I didn't know my grandparents' unconditional love
would stay unconditional,
taking me & my sister to Vegas to celebrate my 21st birthday
where they'd see me as the woman I am for the first time,
and welcome me with arms stretched wider than angel wings.

I didn't think I could cry about that, but I do.
Because one thing I definitely didn't know about being trans
is that you can be unapologetically yourself
and people, your friends, your families,
will still love you
like a victory.

lessons from becoming a "post-op transsexual"

1

it's not your gender or body that makes you dysphoric
it's looking like your parents

2

becoming pretty makes it easier for folks to fuck you
but harder for them to see you
and arduous for you to trust them

3

you're not allowed to say it, but fuck it—
you're gonna miss the soft, quick growth of your beard
and the clothes and makeup quirks that made you weird

4

though everyone said you were beautiful & lovable before
you didn't experience it until now

5

being mistaken for cis
isn't safe

6

the greatest gift of shapeshifting
is having fresh skin and novel sex
that doesn't feel at all like rape

7

being fucked and loved and treated nicely
doesn't stop you from wanting to kill yourself

8

if you don't grow your own roots
someone else will invite you into their soil
and rot you

9

you deserve more than frosting

10

you learn to leave healthy relationships
because non-abusiveness doesn't mean
love

Life Is Hard So I Made This List Of Gratitudes

(for Aurelia Mercer)

i am grateful for ube ice cream, tres leches cake, and Lactaid
for my tarot deck's impeccably intuitive sharp tongue
for 15 minute naps between classes before the alarm goes off

i am grateful for my love and care toward myself
using a cell phone, my thumbs, and vulnerability
to send those terrifying texts asking to quiet my suicidal thoughts
making those impossible phone calls when i need
just a few minutes
to last a lifetime longer

Can you not hate me for 5 minutes?
which means
please, love me a bit louder
remind me why we chose & choose each other

tell me about that time we went to the beach
my hair mermaid hues
your grin vast as ocean
scorching sand singeing toes
body surfing in icy sea
where we swear we felt a sea lion
kiss our bellies, imbue with blessings

or, the time we spent three days in bed
eating pepinos, takis, fruit salads, and lemon chicken
marinating in burning sage and hot wax
massaging the toxic out of us
to dream in peace

i am grateful for high-rise beds i can hide under
high-tides that carry hope and starfish
high nights watching Parks & Rec with mint chocolate Milanos

the sisterhood of the traveling altar
filled with care-packaged crisis & birthday gifts
that picks up snow, hair, jewelry, and herbs
from every city and state i tumble through

i am grateful i chose to stay alive
to fill my bones with resolution
and my spirit with stubbornness
to show none of me is leaving anywhere

Crying Crystals

my spirit starved for 19 years
famished magic seeking food
i find aroma by instinct

draw a bath seasoned with lavender & bruja oils
stirring witches brew with rose quartz, onyx, & amethyst
marinate me with miracles
then boil my body cleansed

this spirit's mouth an alligator
devouring every magic morsel
crying crystals from generational dams
that held every hurt that turned their corpse to stone

Suicide Squad

 i will lose my mind
because that's what minds do
get lost wandering
to when and where
we rather not

 i will lose my hope
like my bio fam lost me
suddenly, without warning
running, sneaking into tiny places
a mouse couldn't find a crumb in

 i will lose everything
yet, i will gain it back with interest
a dozen beloveds feeding me hand-to-mouth
driving me to psych appointments
reminding me to breathe
damn near brushing my teeth
force feeding me faith and love
not giving up, not going away
not letting crushing thoughts crush me empty
sleeping in their beds
dozing in their backseats
lungs full of redwoods and songs
sobbing in tubs and laps and traffic
laughing at my own bad jokes
snacks and sweets littered across the floor

fucked up horror movies & sardonic comedies

phone calls & text messages all hours of the day

the true Suicide Squad

left not a moment unloved or unwanted

saved a dying girl's life

by loving her, simply

loving me

how to save yourself after no one else does

suffocate on your heart
stretch your skin across the ceiling
stare at scars smiling wide as you lie inanimate
in bed for the seventh consecutive day

take a deep breath of acid into your bones
an anchor of trauma dragging you deep
drowning in virulent memories

buy a disposable camera from the drug store
take snapshots over two months with chosen fam
keep your joy, your own gift of surprise
tape the memories above your dreams

pen ink spell where you want to cut
seven letters, two words, one goal
don't die

take a deep inhale into your heart
another, another, sweet dying fighter

eventually you fill with vigor

smoky quartz vanishing act

don't look at me
i'm not that pretty
under this makeup & tuck
a sheath of heat
bright blinding anxiety
racing thoughts & sweaty brow
a bladder ticking every hour
restless hands, fidgeting fingers
saliva thick rancid sludge
no water no safety no peace—
don't look at me
i'm scared you'll see the treasure of my beauty
rob me of my sacred
leave an empty chest
untucked bare-faced scruffy girl
slamming smoky quartz against thoughts
a cloud of blood & bone
vanishing girl safe in her escape

don't drink his water

I can broadcast that the well is poisoned
but The Girls will drown for its taste
jumping down the cobblestone
with no rope, no pail
maybe a friend, maybe some dope.
feet first into the sludge enveloping them
stripping them of mermaid tails and joy
filling their voids with passionate heartbreak
promises like grease stains, ugly and tarnishing

Girls, trust me.
or rather, trust the well to tell you
hell can be a place or it can be a feeling
both of which are ephemeral
if you would just fucking leave him lonely

survivor femmes who get revenge

this is your awards ceremony
for gutting the men who raped you
stretching their intestines down like red carpet
squishing your way up to the podium to seize
the prize of an urn of their ashes &
an end to your suffering

survivor femmes,
anointed with honor & adoration
through bloody screams
adorned in skin dresses and bone jewelry
that chatter in dismay at your victory
admired for the disgraceful ways you healed
snatching apologies when none were offered

our whispers across the planet will
keep them from victimizing
our hexes will conjure black widow fiends
that immobilize them as we take
tasers and shotguns to their genitals
knives and barbed wire across their eyeballs
nailing their gaslighting tongues to the oven
and burning those lies at 450 degrees
in 30 minute increments for eternity

survivor femmes,
i will not absolve you for you have not sinned
i will build a pantheon in honor of all your crimes
a sanctuary for crazy deranged unpretty revenge
with marble fountains that only drink abusive blood
for future femmes to sacrifice their ills

how to move on

every time you want to call them
count backwards from thirty-seven
then add to the letter you won't mail

keep a bowl made of apache tear
next to your bed for those midnight
possessions of grief to spill into

though they've already crawled underneath
other people, it doesn't mean you need
someone crawling into you

you'll want to be Gwen Stefani *Cool*
but it's okay to be
My, Myself, and I

learn to lick your wrists,
ankles, belly, and breasts
like you used to let them

for every wish to cease breath
call a friend to braid
fresh lavender into your hair

paint your nails a color you enjoy chipping off
go to a karaoke bar
and sing until you're someone else

turn off your psychic
stop reading your horoscope
and fly unknowing for a while

escape to a waterfall
slice your own hair off
throw it to the nymphs

bathe in new beginnings

remember,
your love is a jar of honey
shut tight for genuine eros & kindred

how i fell in love with my ugly

the first time i truly saw myself
brown face, abyss dark eyes, wide nose & fat lips
was my first year of college while
high on shrooms staring at this beautiful broken bruja in the dorm
bathroom

i told her i loved her, & smiled loudly
showing all those stained crowded teeth
that left no space for self-loathing

loving myself didn't make me beautiful
it made me uglier
gave me that invincible courage & coldness
to not listen to the glares as i strutted around
with my learning curve makeup & ashy foundation

embracing ugly magnetized other beauties
who spent time in their ugly
accepted it as truth and didn't seek validation

ugly bitches invented the mirror
to admire ourselves when no one else does

my ugly is a shield, audacious
a sign of the deepest affection and the greatest gift
that countless lineages left legacies of hideous power
for the deserving unsightly to wield

in the quiet, in the calm

last week i sold my car and 3DS for some quick cash
paid my storage unit and ate good
no plan for next month but hey,
these feet will take me those miles until they break off

i nearly killed myself again
the first time in four years it got this bad
i'm not sure why, but my shark auntie said
sometimes having four walls and a door that locks
unleashes all those welled up feelings inside you

my life has been a shitstorm of knives and lovers
all these scars and exes and complicated messes
left in the drought, the Valley, behind those dead hills
with the Jesus Saves lights and stop-and-go traffic

i am near ocean and blown by wind, a new storm of
refreshing beginnings and safe exploration
a land of techies and broken promises that
i'm old enough to walk away from, and instead
towards the darkening horizon,
calm and peaceful

this isn't the eye of the storm, it's the aftermath
picking up my ribcage, mending my baby clothes
forgetting lovers but keeping their bloodied debris of lessons
planting lavender and ivy that will flourish for once

i spend a few weeks in bed, eating snacks and nightmares
somehow get a job at a gelato joint, enough stability
to get my finger & toe nails painted, a few new outfits,
& a half dozen books by QTPOC writers who are alive

things don't feel perfect and my orgasm is still bruised,
my bio family is an amputation heart scar, my hopes are
like baby chicks that fell out the nest dazed and nearly dead,
but there's a heartbeat, a wind, and a direction,
there's a bedroom filled with fotos and art from loved ones,
living in a city where people don't give a shit,
but they give a shit about you.

Midnight Litany

(for Mark Aguhar)

1. these scars as beautiful as they are permanent

2. your pain is more important than how you heal it

3. lovable wanted necessary needed

4. home is in the hurt and happiness

5. earth and your body want you alive

6. growth requires imperfection

7. love the dead love the living love the in-between

8. ugliness is an honor

9. exist as your imagination

10. make love with your spirit and your demons
(give birth to magic)

11. sleep in peace

Fates and Futures

[Image description: A nude pregnant trans woman looks down at the clearly defined, all black orb shape of their lower belly. Their skin is shaded with contour lines. One thick dark braid curves around the right side of their body. A machete is braided into their hair, the handle emerging at the highest point of their head, above their jaw. Their eyes are closed, their eyebrows are made of short dark overlapping strokes, and the same hair pattern covers their chin and jawline, armpits and inner thighs. A small snake curls into a tight S shape over their mouth, and curves down to the center of their chest and toward the right breast. One hand is cupping this breast from below. Their nipples are black and radiate short dark strokes of hair.

Bright cracks spread outward from the body of the snake on their chest. The figure's other arm holds the lower edge of the belly with a hand that has long, white, stiletto shaped nails. On either side of the pregnant belly, three feathers float. Above the belly, a geometric sun radiates upward to meet the cracks coming from the snake on the chest. Below the belly, the flesh of the person's genitals extends downward. Round cloudlike shapes are visible on both sides of the flesh, and a crescent moon with visible craters rests on the right side. Short dark lines of hair extend along the edge of the clouds. The person's hips widen and narrow in bumpy curves and then taper down to the thighs. At the base of the thighs, two large black handprints are placed angling outward. Above them, smaller black handprints climb vertically up the thigh, three on the left side and five on the right side.]

Zaylani

your first skin, sticky placenta and blood
i hold you against me
cherishing nine months of magic and miracle
that stirred within my hopeful womb

my boobs swelled with agave for your suckling hunger
our bonding instincts that we know and need another
your fingers grasping the secrets off my tongue
my arms holding your spine and future

my first true love, my baby feels like
a caressing of my spirit who carries legacy
of lavender, brown skin, and mysticism

your first scream is one that opens your wings wide
a phoenix emerging from all our family's ashes
making peace, becoming salvation
healing child of grace

if we choose this

(for Andrew)

At the Arby's behind your apartment
holding hands across a greasy table and curly fries, you said,
"When I think about having a kid, I think about
who I want the other half of them to be.
I want that half to be you."

One half
crazy perfect bitch
forgiving, relentless, laughing
making it work, making it thrive
prepared with spells & faith
filled with honey & almond chocolates
stubborn righteousness & ideas
a genius by birthright
a legacy by practice

One half
curious perfect badass
forgiving, careful, chuckling
making it better, making it best
prepared with plans & logistics
filled with maple & coffee crisps
stubborn righteousness & ideas
a genius by birthright
a legacy by practice

One whole Jamaican-Mexican-Canadian-Athabaskan-British
Black-brown being created by a year-long decision
of a loving companionship that promised to
raise this gift with gentle compassion,
honor, respect,
and love.

as your mother

i promise

you will smell like soil
sunlight, and syrup

i promise

you will mutate meticulously
effortlessly

i promise

you will be the first spring bloom
to ever halt war

lemongrass

(for Mikey)

this scent you wore heavy
winter and summer 2014
i spent a year seeking it
surprise-finding it in a gifted care package

it sits on the bookshelf adjacent to the headboard
hope in every whiff i'll fall asleep dreaming of the wearer

Caribbean Girl
soul & spirit lover
make home in my nose and memory
the scent sweet as our first and last kiss

how you hold me with a scarf and oil
how i wish i had taken more time, clothes, & touch

will we ever reunite?
planets who cross once in a human's lifetime
make immense magic and lonely endings

i cast a spell to turn my marrow into mulch
nourishing lemongrass 'til harvest come
hoping my essence is laid across your skin

Amoriga

(for Chillóna)

forever is a truth

forever
our limbs holding our spirits
finding matching vibrations
filled with past lives of touch & love

how many times have we found each other
tracing glyphs into hands
hiding kisses in irises, secrets in places
only we can reach in each other,
    like sacred tears only our tongues have the taste buds to know
    seeing our past selves, that ancestral familiarity

you are family   you are lover
both of us born into new heritage
    to mix our love in many bodies & lineages
    the kind of brujería that cherishes chillónas,
    madness & empathy

we had babies all over this world
we grew rainforests and farms
we found the cure to aloneness by filling everything with
    blood, honey, and patience

amoriga, this type of forever —
friendship stronger than partnership
love deeper than marriage

you are an infinite truth i'll remember in every future body

home, mi casa

fresh pan dulce

woven basket full of fruit

a cabinet of tinctures

chosen familia around the dinner table

full bellied laughter

care in surplus

love in abundance, always

scent-free laundry detergent

incense and bruja oils when and where safe

garden flooded in moonlight

spiders & butterflies & hummingbirds & beetles & bees

snakes, few puppies, couple kitties, soft bunnies

rice milk & free range eggs, homemade pickles & preserves

maíz tortillas made with memory-heavy hands

patience by nature, not virtue

children with too many parents

pregnant trans women

breast-feeding trans women

mamá trans women

movie nights con limón popcorn y tajín y chile

labels all over en español y nahuatl for the kidlets

movement art and fotos of our transcestors on every wall

bedrooms in their inhabitants' favorite colors

hand holding and hugs

brown skin basking in sunshine

the feeling of too good to be true

because it is both too good and the truth

brown girl desired

are you an adventurer?
can you climb tree bark
tree trunk, tree branch
to caress mangos without plucking?
savor scent
sweet sap
leaking through throbbing crevice
a taste
a touch
crawl on fingers through coastal sand
dig 'til you curl seashells
crab shells & sand dollars
screaming ocean obscenities & siren songs
a sound
a sight
brown girl limbs tucked
folded small like paper stars
all beauty & sharp angles
intimidates soft fingers that won't
cut a rose from its bush
brown girl blessed skin
beckons & moans

My favorite kind of lesbian sex

you want dirty hot whispers
                    thongs and fishnets
                              wet pussies & trembling thighs

i want lipstick stained pillow cases
                    moaning louder than birth
                              orgasms Aphrodite couldn't trademark

we want mermaid seafoam hard and far
                    awash our bodies in sea salt
                              tasting ocean between each other's breasts

fucking each other the way girls with dicks have been
    warned not to

        i love you in the erotic embodiment of all your fantasies

          cum to bed, babe
                be the high tide pulling in
                        soaking my parched beach sand

Mexican Sex

Panocha pan dulce dry
we need abuelita's recipe for hot chocolate
ancestral hot sweet cinnamon drink
perfected over generations
nuestros tías y mamás y abuelas
want us to feel the creation of magic
taught us how to braid hair to
tie each other up against the headboard
con Virgen de Guadalupe's portrait above the bed
blessing us with every orgasm she's dreamt about

We were taught to wear red
the hue our melanin mates best with
color of blood & love & magic moons
all the elements you taste in my cunt

Snake fang mi corazón amor
i'll sword su boca
take turns slapping nalgas
road head in low riders down Highway 1 during dusk
our chichis kissed by sky
brown nipples large in the face of biting winds

Making love is liberation
liberate me mamas
liberate me all night

Catalyst

(for Toni Luna)

if we're all made of stars
i'm the spark that explodes you, and
the dark matter that encompasses your brightness

i'm the cliffs that hold your oceanic rage
the tide pools that grow your creatures, and
the current your wings seek to soar with

i am that moment when you come out to yourself
when you finish undergrad after three psychotic breakdowns, and
when your first said they loved you

i'm that feeling when the rollercoaster dives
that final stutter-breath after sobbing, and
when you have your favorite orgasm

i am what you seek in therapy
knees bent praying for miracles
every coin-flipped wish into a fountain

if i am your catalyst
keep me, contain me, hold me still
prove a love that is greater than my power

THE GIRLS ARE GODS

THE GIRLS ARE GODS
GODDESSES, GODDEXES
HAIRY AND TOWERING AND
BROAD SHOULDERED AND WIDE
WITH MAHOGANY VOICES
TIGHT TUCKS AND 5 O'CLOCK SHADOWS
FIERCE AND FLY AND FUNNY AND FEROCIOUS
FILLED WITH ENVY AND STEEL AND HONEY AND LUST

THE GIRLS ARE GODS
GODDESSES, GODDEXES
VOGUE QUEENS & BUTCH QUEENS & STEALTH QUEENS
NEW YORK TIME BEST SELLERS & RED CARPET ROYALTY
WHISPER NETWORK DOCTORS & FASHION WEEK ORIGINS
SLY NONPROFIT MAGICIANS & SHY STREET HUSTLERS

THE GIRLS ARE GODS
GODDESSES, GODDEXES
STOMPING SERENADING PROPHESIZING FLYING
CRYING RESISTING REJOICING DESTROYING
SHAPING THE WORLD THROUGH THEIR NAILS
THROUGH LIPSTICKED LIPS SPITTING SPELLS

THE GIRLS ARE SUNS
WHO WERE SONS
WHO FOUND OUT TRUE FAMILIA
NEVER LEAVES YOU COMPROMISING, SILENT, OR ALONE

THE GIRLS ARE
ORIGINAL SHAPESHIFTERS
DAUGHTERS OF STONEWALL
MOTHERS OF FEMME FUTURES
DIVINE FEMININITY
GODS
GODDESSES
AND GODDEXES

letter from me in 2050

hey laurel,

in this timeline, you change your name once more.
you get The Surgery, but it's not the one you think.
it's one where you can store all your memories in a—
what would you call it then? a hard drive, i think—
and you can show it to your therapist who then
facilitates your pain to the New Planet and exchanges
it for Hinahoy, which is a new emotion we created
when we took trauma victim's misery and mixed it
with a bunch of herbal remedies. it's complicated,
but as a soil user you'll understand it in a few decades.

i can't tell you life gets better, or what not to do, because knowing us,
you'll do the same shit anyway.
life's okay, sometimes it's not, but i know you need reassurance. i'll tell
you three things, only because they're things our heredity has
relentlessly tried to break for centuries.

first,
you'll stop loving the people who don't love you.

second,
your path is wildly yours. the technology and
magic we use today was unknown to you then. there
will still be times where death offers the best alternative,
but i promise you we find a way. our life is important.

third,

you will have a baby who is nothing like you dreamt of, who terrifies you in how they mirror the best parts of your beauty, mannerisms, and personality without any of the trauma or complication we were resistant to love, who beams brighter than the ginormous Milky Way sun you know, and who deeply & truly loves — *loves!* — you with gratitude.

hold onto that.

from your future liberated self,
laurel l.r.s.

p.s. you have lots of great sex after celibacy.
it's so fucking worth the wait.

About the Author

Luna Merbruja is a Mexican-Athabaskan multidisciplinary artist and writer based in the San Francisco Bay Area. They are the author of *Trauma Queen* and *Heal Your Love*. They have written for *Autostraddle* and *Everyday Feminism*, and have been published in *Nerve Endings: The New Trans Erotic* and *The Resilience Anthology*.

For more information, visit: www.luna.merbruja.com.

Lightning Source UK Ltd.
Milton Keynes UK
UKHW01f1837040918
328333UK00002B/607/P